Catholic Update
guide to
Mary

Mary Carol Kendzia,
Series Editor

Franciscan
MEDIA
Cincinnati, Ohio

RESCRIPT

In accord with the *Code of Canon Law*, I hereby grant my *Imprimatur* the *Catholic Update Guide to Mary* by Mary Carol Kendzia, series editor.
Most Reverend Joseph R. Binzer
Vicar General and Auxiliary Bishop
of the Archdiocese of Cincinnati
Cincinnati, Ohio
June 3, 2013

The *Imprimatur* ("Permission to Publish") is a declaration that a book or pamphlet is considered to be free from doctrinal or moral error. It is not implied that those who have granted the *Imprimatur* agree with the contents, opinions or statements expressed.

Scripture passages have been taken from *New Revised Standard Version Bible*, copyright ©1989 by the Division of Christian Education of the National Council of the Churches of Christ in the U.S.A., and used by permission. All rights reserved.

Cover and book design by Mark Sullivan
Cover image © istockphoto | Stephanie Asher

LIBRARY OF CONGRESS CATALOGING-IN-PUBLICATION DATA
Catholic update guide to Mary / [edited by] Mary Carol Kendzia.
      pages cm.—(Catholic update guides)
Summary: "This simple yet comprehensive resource offers a concise overview of Mary, one of the most popular figures in all of Catholicism. It looks at the Mary of history, whose life is intertwined with the mystery of Jesus. It will reconstruct a picture that is quite different from the pious images to which so many of us are accustomed, and guide us to connect through her to her son, Jesus. The guide will show us the depth and breadth of how we see and approach Mary and remind us of how she has a special place in the liturgical life of the Church"— Provided by publisher.
    Includes bibliographical references.
    ISBN 978-1-61636-672-8 (pbk.)
 1. Mary, Blessed Virgin, Saint. 2. Catholic Church—Doctrines. I. Kendzia, Mary Carol.
      BT603.C38 2013
      232.91—dc23
                                                                      2013018834

ISBN 978-1-61636-672-8

Copyright ©2013, Franciscan Media. All rights reserved.
Published by Franciscan Media
28 W. Liberty St.
Cincinnati, OH 45202
www.FranciscanMedia.org

Printed in the United States of America.
Printed on acid-free paper.
13 14 15 16 17   5 4 3 2 1

Contents

About This Series v

Introduction vii

Chapter One
The Historical Mary 1

Chapter Two
Mary's Importance to Our Faith 12

Chapter Three
Images of Mary 19

Chapter Four
Feasts of Mary 26

Chapter Five
Praying the Rosary 35

Chapter Six
Other Prayers to Mary 47

Sources 51

Contributors 52

About This Series

The Catholic Update guides take the best material from our bestselling newsletters and videos to bring you up-to-the-minute resources for your faith. Topically arranged for these books, the words you'll find in these pages are the same clear, concise, authoritative information you've come to expect from the nation's most trusted faith formation series. Plus, we've designed this series with a practical focus—giving the "what," "why," and "how to" for the people in the pews.

The series takes the topics most relevant to parish life—e.g., the Mass, sacraments, Scripture, the liturgical year—and draws them out in a fresh and straightforward way. The books can be read by individuals or used in a study group. They are an invaluable resource for sacramental preparation, RCIA participants, faith formation, and liturgical ministry training, and are a great tool for everyday Catholics who want to brush up on the basics.

The content for the series comes from noted authors such as Thomas Richstatter, O.F.M., Lawrence Mick, Leonard Foley, O.F.M., Carol Luebering, William H. Shannon, and others. Their theology and approach is grounded in Catholic practice and tradition, while mindful of current Church practice and teaching. We blend each author's style and approach into a voice that is clear, unified, and eminently readable.

Enrich your knowledge and practice of the Catholic faith with the helpful topics in the Catholic Update Guide series.

Mary Carol Kendzia
Series Editor

Introduction

The history of Christian devotion to the Blessed Mother encompasses many ways of seeing her: as handmaid, as model of liberation, as mother, as healer, as queen, to name but a few. Throughout the ages, the people of God have shown her veneration and love. They have called upon her in prayer and they imitate her.

But what do we really know about the woman whom we call "Mother of God" and "Mother of the Church," the "first of all the saints," the "model believer"? What do contemporary Scripture studies, archaeological research, and analysis of the literature of her time reveal to us about Mary? What does our prayer to Mary and our celebration of feasts to Mary reveal to us about her and ourselves as a people of faith in her Son as Savior?

The *Catholic Update Guide to Mary* looks at the Mary of history, whose life is so intertwined with the mystery of Jesus. It will reconstruct a picture that is quite different from the pious images to which so many of us are accustomed, conditioned as they are by beautiful portraits of medieval artists, the serene rhapsodies of musicians and poets. It offers us an invitation to understand and explore how Mary is important to our faith, how we can more richly pray to Mary and celebrate Mary's role in our lives.

Every century and culture has interpreted Mary in different ways. Consider the paintings, sculptures, icons, music, liturgies, feasts, spiritual writings, theologies, official doctrines over the centuries. It seems that the image of Mary has allowed the Christian imagination to think very creatively and in different ways about Mary. But as the generation alive today, how should we consider Mary in the twenty-first century?

As the Mother of Christ, she is the morning star announcing the rising of the Sun of Righteousness. Like the moon at the dawn of a new day, she is wholly bathed in the glory of the sun that is to come after her. Her beauty is a reflection of his.

The glories of Mary have only gradually been discovered by the Church during nearly two thousand years of study and contemplation. The basic lines of Catholic Mariology (theology of Mary) are by now beyond dispute, enshrined as they are in the Scriptures; in the liturgy; in prayer, poetry, song, and art; in the writings of saints and theologians; and in the teaching of popes and councils. Mary holds a secure place as the greatest of the saints, conceived and born without original sin and free from actual sin at any point in her life.

Full of grace, she is exemplary in her faith, hope, love of God, and generous concern for others. Having virginally conceived the Son of God in her womb, she remained a virgin throughout her life. At the end of her earthly sojourn she was taken up body and soul into heaven, where she continues to exercise her spiritual motherhood and to intercede for the needs of her children on earth. This body of

Introduction

teaching, constructed laboriously over long centuries, belongs inalienably to the patrimony of the Church and can scarcely be contested from within the Catholic tradition.

Mary becomes for us someone to help us look at our lives, to show us who we are, to help us become ourselves, and to live fully. In turning with devotion to the "real life" of the Mother of God, in seeing how Mary lived by faith, we might find the courage and grace to do the same, united with her.

The importance of Mary's role is seen in the esteem and honor Pope John Paul II placed before her. In his apostolic letter *Rosarium Virginis Mariae* (The Rosary of the Virgin Mary) published in October 2002, John Paul II spoke of the "wondrous presence of the Mother of God in the mystery of Christ and the Church," and pointed to the rosary as "my favorite prayer, marvelous in its simplicity and its depth."

Mary, the Mother of God, is our mother, too. Just as Mary gave us Jesus through God's grace, so Jesus in turn gave Mary to the Church when he said to the beloved disciple, "Here is your mother" (John 19:27).

CHAPTER ONE

The Historical Mary

We know very little about Mary (or Miriam, as she would be known in Hebrew) of Nazareth as an actual historical person. In this she is in solidarity with the multitudes of those through the centuries, especially poor women and poor men, whose lives are considered not worth recording.

The four Gospels portray her in very different ways, reflecting their very different theologies. At first glance, Mark comes across as having a somewhat negative view of Jesus's Mother. She arrives with other members of the family as Jesus is preaching, and they call to him. When the crowd tells Jesus his Mother is asking for him, he replies, "Who are my mother and my brothers?... Whoever does the will of God is my brother and sister and mother" (see Mark 3:31–35). And Mary remains outside.

Matthew's view of Mary is rather neutral by comparison. He places her in the genealogy of the messiah, in line with four other women who act outside the patriarchal marriage structure, thereby becoming unexpectedly God's partners in a promise-and-fulfillment schema. In Matthew's Gospel, though, Mary doesn't speak, and all the focus on the birth story is around Joseph.

Luke describes Mary as a woman of faith, overshadowed by the Spirit at Jesus's conception and at the beginning of the Church at Pentecost. She is the first to respond to the glad tidings to hear the word of God and keep it. It's a very positive view of Mary, from which most of our tradition has come.

Finally, John has a highly stylized portrayal of the Mother of Jesus, and that's all he ever calls her. He never names her. She is mentioned twice in John's Gospel, at the beginning and at the end, at Cana and at the cross. And again, she is there embodying responsive discipleship to the Word made flesh.

The Annunciation: The Angel's Message to Mary

> In the sixth month the angel Gabriel was sent by God to a town in Galilee called Nazareth, to a virgin engaged to a man whose name was Joseph, of the house of David. The virgin's name was Mary. (Luke 1:26–27)

What was Mary's life like before she learned that she was to become the mother of Israel's messiah? While Luke's Gospel does not offer a lot of information about the Mother of Jesus, it does tell us three important details that allow us to catch a glimpse of Mary's life before the angel Gabriel visited.

First, we learn that she lives in Nazareth, a small village in the region of Galilee. Jesus's coming from such an obscure village will cause him trouble later in his public ministry. Some will question how he really could be sent from God, since no prophet ever came out of this region (see John 7:52), while others will wonder whether anything good at all could come out of this little town (see John 1:46).

Second, Luke describes Mary as betrothed to Joseph. In first-century Judaism, betrothal was the first step of a two-stage marriage process. At her betrothal Mary would have consented before public witnesses to marry Joseph, and this would have established the couple as husband and wife. As a betrothed wife, however, Mary would have continued to live with her own family, apart from her husband, for up to a year. Only after this period of betrothal would the second stage of marriage take place—the consummation of the marriage and the wife's moving into the husband's home.

Consequently, as a betrothed woman, Mary still would have been living with her family in Nazareth. As such, it makes sense that Luke would describe her at this stage as "a virgin." Perhaps even more noteworthy, however, is the fact that women in first-century Palestine generally were betrothed in their early teen years. This tells us that Mary probably was a very young woman when God called her to serve as the mother of the messiah.

Finally, the most striking point we know about Mary's life prior to the Annunciation is that she married a man from "the house of David" (Luke 1:27). This small detail indicates that Mary became part of the most famous family in all of Israel: King David's family.

Yet, in the time of Mary and Joseph, the Jews are suffering under Roman occupation. In such oppressive conditions, being a member of David's family no longer holds the privileges, authority, and honor that it held in the glory days of the kings who reigned in Jerusalem. Instead, this Joseph "of the house of David" is a humble carpenter, leading a quiet, ordinary life a small rural town.

Full of Grace, the Lord Is with You
Mary's world radically changes when the angel Gabriel appears to her saying, "Hail, full of grace, the Lord is with you!" Understandably, Mary "was greatly troubled." She is not startled simply by the angel itself but by the angel's greeting: "But she was much perplexed by his words and pondered what sort of greeting this might be" (see Luke 1:28–29).

No one else in the Bible has ever been honored by an angel with such an exalted title as "full of grace." The Greek word *kecharitomene*, which here is translated "full of grace," indicates that Mary already possesses God's saving grace, making her a pure and holy temple in which the divine Christ child will dwell for nine months.

Second, the angel says, "The Lord is with you," words used in the Old Testament to signal that someone was being called to a daunting task. In fact, these words often accompanied an invitation from God to play a crucial role in his plan of salvation. With these words, Mary probably realizes that a lot is being asked of her. Yet she will not have to face these difficulties alone. God will give her the one thing she needs most: the assurance that he will be with her.

Third, we learn more of Mary's mission in Luke 1:30, as the angel says, "Do not be afraid, Mary, for you have found favor with God." The notion of finding "favor with God" also would bring to mind Old Testament covenant mediators in God's salvation plan. Like these great covenant mediators of the Old Testament, Mary has found favor with God. Walking in the footsteps of Noah, Abraham, Moses, and David, Mary now is called to serve as an important cooperator in the divine plan to bring salvation to all the nations.

What Child Is This?

> "And now, you will conceive in your womb and bear a son, and you will name him Jesus. He will be great, and will be called the Son of the Most High, and the Lord God will give to him the throne of his ancestor David. He will reign over the house of Jacob forever, and of his kingdom there will be no end." (Luke 1:31–33)

Now the angel Gabriel gets to the heart of his message and the nature of Mary's mission: Mary will bear a son who will bring Israel's history to its climax. She will be the mother of Israel's long-awaited messiah-king.

These themes—the throne of David, greatness, sonship, an everlasting kingdom—make the angel's message to Mary quite clear: Mary will have the long-awaited royal Son who will fulfill the dynastic promises God made to David (see 2 Samuel 7:9, 12–14, 16).

It is important to note that up to this point of the angel's announcement, there has been no explicit mention of the child's divine origins. Also, there has been no explicit mention yet of a miraculous virgin birth. Presumably, if Mary were like most first-century betrothed women, she would anticipate conceiving of this child through the natural means of marital relations after her betrothal period ended and after she moved in with her husband.

However, Mary surprisingly asks, "How shall this be, since I have no husband?" Only now does Gabriel underscore the extraordinary type of motherhood to which Mary is being called: "The Holy Spirit will come upon you, and the power of the Most High will overshadow you; therefore the child to be born will be called holy, the Son of God."

How will Mary, who is betrothed and still a virgin, bear a child? By the spirit and power of God, Gabriel says. Here we have the first clear indication of the virginal conception of the messiah.

Furthermore, we see that Jesus's filial relationship with God far surpasses that of any king in David's dynasty. Jesus will be called Son of God not simply because of his role as Davidic heir and messiah but because of his unique divine origin. Gabriel tells Mary that she will conceive through God's extraordinary intervention of sending the Holy Spirit upon her, and this is the reason for calling him God's Son.

Early Christians saw Mary's conceiving Jesus by the power of the Holy Spirit as an important sign of Christ's humanity and divinity. On one hand, it points to his divine nature by highlighting his unique divine origin and her as the Mother of her God. On the other hand, the Church fathers also saw the virginal conception as a sign that the divine Son of God really became human, taking the flesh of his mother Mary.

Mary's Fiat

Consider all that has happened to Mary in this brief encounter with Gabriel. First, an angel visits the young woman from the small town of Nazareth. This alone would have been quite startling. Second, in hearing the angel's words, "The Lord is with you" and "You have found favor with God," Mary probably realizes that God is calling her to some daunting task.

Third, she finds out that she will be expecting a baby. Fourth, she is informed that this child just happens to be the long-awaited messiah who will restore Israel's kingdom and bring the history of the world to its climactic moment. Fifth, she will conceive of this child not through natural means but through a miraculous conception brought about by God's Holy Spirit. Finally, the angel tells her that this child is the divine Son of God.

It is difficult to imagine what Mary was going through in those brief moments. While we don't know much about Mary's emotions and thoughts at the angel's annunciation, the one response Luke does record for us is one of complete trust: "Then Mary said, 'Here am I, the servant of the Lord; let it be with me according to your word'" (Luke 1:38).

What is interesting about Mary's response is that "let it be with me" expresses not a passive acceptance but a joyful wishing or desiring on Mary's part. She positively desires it and fully embraces God's call for her to serve as the mother of the messiah.

The Earliest Christian: A Model Disciple

Many scholars—Catholic and Protestant alike—recognize Mary as the first Christian disciple and a model follower of Jesus. Her husband, Joseph, seems to have died before Jesus's public ministry began. We know that Mary herself, however, lived through the time of that ministry (see Mark 3:31; John 2:1–12).

In Luke's Gospel, Jesus says that those who hear the word of God and keep it are blessed and are included in his family of disciples (see Luke 8:21). Mary fits this description better than anyone else in Luke's Gospel. From the very beginning she accepts God's word from the angel Gabriel and calls herself the servant of the Lord. In subsequent scenes we will see that Mary responds promptly to her relative Elizabeth's needs as soon as she learns from Gabriel that Elizabeth is pregnant in her old age.

Furthermore, she is counted among the "blessed" disciples in Luke's Gospel. Not only will Elizabeth call Mary blessed for believing God's word (1:45), but Mary herself will say that all generations will call her blessed (1:48). Similarly, like a good disciple who hears God's word and keeps it, Mary will "keep in her heart" the angel's joyous message at Jesus's birth (2:19) and his words to her when she finds him in the Temple (2:51).

John tells us that Mary was present at Jesus's crucifixion (John 19:25–27), though the other evangelists are silent about this. At that time she was probably close to fifty years old, well beyond the age at which most women in that era died. She lived on at least into the early days of the Church.

Luke states that she was in the Upper Room in Jerusalem with the eleven remaining apostles, "devoting themselves to prayer, together with certain women, including Mary…as well as his brothers" (Acts 1:14). The lovely paintings and icons of Pentecost that picture the Spirit descending on Mary and the apostles hardly do justice to Luke's text in Acts 1:15, which indicates that she was there with a community of 120 persons following her Son's resurrection and ascension into heaven.

After Pentecost, Mary disappears from history. The rest of her life is shrouded in legend. She may well have died as a member of the Jerusalem community, though a later tradition portrays her as moving to Ephesus in the company of the apostle John. There is a shrine there, in modern-day Turkey, honoring that tradition.

Mary as Jewish

Much of this knowledge of the circumstances in which she lived has resulted from the contemporary quest for the historical Jesus, whose life was woven within the political, economic, social, and cultural fabric of first-century Palestine. But it serves us as well for a quest for the historical Mary as a Jewish village woman of faith.

As a member of the people of Israel, Mary inherited the Jewish faith in one living God, stemming from Abraham and Sarah onwards. She prayed to a God who hears the cry of the poor, frees the enslaved Hebrews, and brings them into their covenant relationship.

Given Jesus's clear knowledge and practice of the Jewish faith in his adult life, as reflected in the Gospels, it is reasonable to assume that Mary, with her husband, Joseph, practiced this Jewish religion in their home, following Torah, observing Sabbath and the festivals, reciting prayers, lighting candles, and going to synagogue, according to the custom in Galilee.

Later at the end of Jesus's life, Luke depicts Mary in her older years as a member of the early Jerusalem community. For many years, these "Jewish Christians," these earliest of Christians, proclaimed the Good News to their fellow Jews trying to get them to understand the promise of God has been fulfilled, before finally being persuaded by Paul and others that the Gospel was meant for gentiles, too.

It does no honor to Mary's memory to bleach her of her Jewishness. We've done this ethnically by turning her swarthy Mediterranean, Jewish complexion into fair skin and blonde hair and blue eyes. But we've also done this religiously by turning her deeply rooted Jewish piety into that of a latter-day Catholic. She wasn't.

Mary, a Peasant Woman

What does history tell us? We know that Mary was actually called Miriam, after the sister of Moses. Most likely she was born in Nazareth, a tiny Galilean town of about sixteen hundred people, during the reign of Herod the Great, a violent puppet-king propped up by Roman military might.

In Palestine at that time, women ordinarily married at about age thirteen, in order to maximize childbearing and to guarantee their virginity, so it is likely that Mary's espousal to Joseph (see Matthew 1:18) and the birth of Jesus occurred when she was very young. Luke indicates that Mary gave birth to Jesus during a census required by the Romans around 6 B.C., in a cave or stall where animals were stabled.

A feeding trough served as his crib. This is easy enough to visualize, since even today poor refugees use cardboard boxes as makeshift beds for newborn infants. It would be a mistake to think of Mary as fragile, even at thirteen. As a peasant woman capable of walking the hill country of Judea while pregnant, of giving birth in a stable, of making a four- or five-day journey on foot to Jerusalem once a year or so, of sleeping in the open country like other pilgrims, and of engaging in daily hard labor at home, she probably had a robust physique in youth and even in her later years.

Nazareth, a Mediterranean rural village, was populated largely by peasants working the land and craftsmen who served their basic needs. The picture of the Holy Family as a tiny group of three living in a tranquil, monastic-like carpenter's shop is highly improbable. Like most people at that time, Joseph, Mary, and Jesus probably lived in an extended family unit, where three or four houses of one or two rooms each were built around an open courtyard, in which relatives shared an oven, a cistern, and a millstone for grinding grain, and where domestic animals also lived.

Like women in many parts of the world today, Mary most likely spent about ten hours a day on domestic chores like carrying water from a nearby well or stream, gathering wood for the fire, cooking meals, and washing utensils and clothes.

Married to the local carpenter, she took care of the household. Who were the members of this extended household? Mark's Gospel speaks of Jesus as "the carpenter, the son of Mary and brother of James and Joses and Judas and Simon, and are not his sisters here with us?" (Mark 6:3). His sisters Mark leaves unnamed, as typically happened with groups of women in the New Testament.

Were these "brothers and sisters" children of Jesus's aunt (see John 19:25) and therefore cousins? Were they Joseph's children by a previous marriage? We do not know their precise relationship to Jesus and Mary, but it is probable that they all lived in close proximity, within the same compound.

Their life was grinding, with a triple-tax burden: to imperial Rome, to King Herod the Great, and to the Temple (to which, traditionally, they owed ten percent of the harvest).

Like other village women of her day, she was probably illiterate. Mary spoke Aramaic, with a Galilean accent (see Matthew 26:73), but she also had contact with a multilingual world. She heard Latin as it slipped from the tongues of Roman soldiers, Greek as it was used in commerce and educated circles, and Hebrew as the Torah was proclaimed in the synagogue.

Questions for Reflection

1. What do you relate from your own life to Mary's journey of faith?
2. When have you fully embraced God's call, even when it meant personal sacrifice?
3. Have you ever felt challenged by friends and family when you acted in accord with your faith?

CHAPTER TWO

Mary's Importance to Our Faith

Mary's authentic and important role in the mystery of Christ is a vital part of the Gospel. The Gospel passages reveal the virgin as a dynamic, grace-filled woman to whom God offered a pivotal and active role in the drama of salvation.

Pope Paul VI in On Devotion to the Blessed Virgin Mary (1974) emphasized that devotion to Mary as "Mother and Associate of the Savior" should be permeated with "the great themes of the Christian message" as we find it in Scripture (On Devotion to the Blessed Virgin, 30). Paul VI called the attention of modern women to the reality that the Mary we hail in the "Ave Maria" was a dynamic, grace-filled woman who gave her "active and responsible consent" to the Incarnation. When she proclaimed her Magnificat by which she responds to Elizabeth's greeting, she announced "that God vindicates the humble and the oppressed and removes the powerful people of this world from their privileged positions" (On Devotion to the Blessed Virgin, 37).

Those who picture Mary as a passive woman uninvolved in the work of forging God's kingdom of justice and peace have not yet encountered the Mary of the Gospels.

When Pope John Paul II survived an assassin's bullet in 1981, he credited his safety to the protection of Mary. The assassination attempt had taken place in St. Peter's Square on May 13, the anniversary of the first appearance of Our Lady to the children at Fatima sixty-four years earlier, in 1917.

Five months later, on the day the pope resumed his public appearances, October 7 (the Feast of the Holy Rosary), he pointed out the connection with Fatima, saying he was "indebted to the Blessed Virgin" and adding, "In everything that happened to me on that very day, I felt that extraordinary motherly protection and care, which turned out to be stronger than the deadly bullet."

Pope John Paul II's Understanding of Mary

Karol Wojtyla, Pope John Paul II, was a devoted son of Mary ever since early youth, when he worshiped at her shrines in the neighborhood of his native Wadowice. During the Nazi occupation of Poland, as a chaplet leader in a "living rosary," he joined in prayers to Mary for peace and liberation.

He emphatically denied that Marian teaching is a devotional supplement to a system of doctrine that would be complete without her. On the contrary, he held, she occupies an indispensable place in the whole plan of salvation. "The mystery of Mary," wrote the pope, "is a revealed truth which imposes itself on the intellect of believers and requires of those in the Church who have the task of studying and teaching a method of doctrinal reflection no less rigorous than that used in all theology."

As a bishop at Vatican II, Wojtyla made several important interventions regarding Mary. He favored the inclusion of Mariology within the Dogmatic Constitution on the Church. Mary, he declared in a written intervention in September 1964, having built up Christ's physical body as mother, continues this role in the mystical body.

The Second Vatican Council did declare in the Dogmatic Constitution on the Church (1964) that "the Catholic Church, taught by the Holy Spirit, honors her with the affection of filial piety as a most loving mother" (53). To the great satisfaction of then-Archbishop Wojtyla, Paul VI that year explicitly proclaimed Mary to be Mother of the Church.

The Pope's Encyclical

The Mariology of John Paul II appears in concentrated form in his encyclical *Redemptoris Mater* (1987) and more diffusely in a series of seventy Wednesday audience catecheses on Mary delivered between 1995 and 1997.

The key term that unifies the pope's Mariology is motherhood. Mary is the Mother of the Redeemer, Mother of Divine Grace, Mother of the Church. The Council of Ephesus in the fifth century established the foundational dogma of Mariology, that Mary is Mother of God, in Greek, *Theotokos* (literally, "God-bearer").

In *Redemptoris Mater*, the pope calls attention to the ecumenical value of this dogma (30–32); Mary's involvement in the saving mission of her Son, beginning with the Annunciation, conceiving through faith, and obedience to the divine Word that came to her from on high (13); and Mary's role not exempt from sorrow.

After the death of Jesus, according to the pope, Mary's motherly office assumes a new form. In saying to the beloved disciple, "Here is your mother," Jesus places the apostles under her maternal care (see John 19:25–27).

There is a mysterious correspondence, Pope John Paul II stressed, in Mary's maternal relationships to Jesus and to the Church. By her unceasing intercession she cooperates with maternal love in the spiritual birth and development of the sons and daughters of the Church (*Redemptoris Mater,* 44). "Choosing her as Mother of all humanity," wrote the pope, "the heavenly Father wanted to reveal the maternal dimension of his divine tenderness and care for men and women of every age."

Besides being an icon of the whole Church, Mary is in a particular way a model for women. The contrasting vocations of virginity and motherhood meet and coexist in her (see John Paul II's 1988 apostolic letter *Mulieris Dignitatem*).

The single, the married, and the widowed can all look to her for inspiration. In Mary women can find an exemplar of "the loftiest sentiments of which the human heart is capable: the self-offering totality of love; the strength that is capable of bearing the greatest sorrows; limitless fidelity and tireless devotion to work; the ability to combine penetrating intuition with words of support and encouragement" (*Redemptoris Mater,* 46).

Mother of Total Life

If Christ had not given us his mother to be our mother, wouldn't we have pined for such a relationship? In recounting her life, St. Teresa of Avila writes: "I remember that when my mother died I was twelve years old or a little less. When I began to understand what I had lost, I went, afflicted, before an image of Our Lady and besought her with many tears to be my mother. It seems to me that although I did this in simplicity it helped me. For I have found favor with this sovereign Virgin in everything I have asked of her, and in the end she has drawn me to herself" (*Collected Works*).

We cannot understand ourselves and be ourselves if we have only ourselves for reference. To be truly ourselves, we need someone else. This conviction is a recurrent theme in the earlier writings of Pope Benedict XVI, then Cardinal Joseph Ratzinger: "[Alone] we cannot come to terms with ourselves. Our I becomes acceptable to us only if it has first become acceptable to another I. We can love ourselves only if we have first been loved by someone else."

> Man is that strange creature that needs not just physical birth but also appreciation if he is to subsist.... If an individual is to accept himself, someone must say to him: 'It is good that you exist'—must say it, not with words, but with that act of the entire being that we call love. For it is the way of love to will the other's existence and, at the same time, to bring that existence forth again. The key to the I lies with the you. (*Principles of Catholic Theology*)

Mary, mother and model of the Church, is given to us to be our way of belonging. In the gift of Mary's motherhood, the Christian welcomes the Mother of God "into his own home." Christ personally hands over his mother to each individual on Calvary in the person of the beloved disciple.

St. Thérèse of Lisieux understood uncannily how this truth applies to our relationship with the Mother of God: "With regard to the Blessed Virgin, I must confide to you one of my simple ways with her: I surprise myself at times by saying to her: 'But good Blessed Virgin, I find I am more blessed than you, for I have you for a mother, and you do not have a Blessed Virgin to love.... It is true you are the mother of Jesus, but this Jesus you have given entirely to us… and he, on the cross, he gave you to us as mother. Thus we are richer than you since we possess Jesus and since you are ours also'" (*General Correspondence*).

Why focus on the historical, Gospel-based Mary? There are three key reasons that lead to greater understanding of Mary's role in our lives:

1. Her history brings her nearer to us. While there is an alluring quality to the gorgeous Madonnas depicted by medieval artists, Mary didn't look like that. This first-century Jewish woman, living in a peasant village, was much more like billions of people today than like the women in those beautiful paintings. Though her culture was quite different from that of our twenty-first century post-industrial society, it was not unlike the hard, daily life of women living under oppressive circumstances in thousands of villages as they exist today in Asia, Africa, and Latin America.

2. She listens to God's word. In fact, her holiness lies in persistent, faithful listening to God's word. As events unfolded around her, she had to figure out continually what God is asking of her. She looks for the word of God in people and events, listens to that word, ponders it, and then acts on it. She doubtless repeats again and again what she said to Gabriel, "May it be done to me according to your word" (Luke 1:38). Day by day she lives a "pilgrimage of faith," to use the words of Vatican II (see *Lumen Gentium,* 58).

3. She sings freedom's song. Today we recognize Mary's Magnificat as a rousing freedom song of the poor. Mary epitomizes those marginalized by society, for whom there is "no place for them in the inn" (Luke 2:7).

The historical Mary experienced poverty, oppression, violence, and the execution of her son. Her faith is deeply rooted in that context. Before the omnipotent God, she recognizes her own "lowly estate." She is not among the world's powerful. She is simply God's "maidservant." But she cries out, in the Magnificat, with gratitude for God's gifts: "My soul magnifies the Lord, and my spirit rejoices in God my Savior."

Questions for Reflection
1. Why should we focus on the historical, Gospel-based Mary?
2. How is Mary a model for women?
3. How can we as Christians welcome Mary into our own homes?

CHAPTER THREE

Images of Mary

Throughout history, Christians and non-Christians alike have looked to Mary as an object of veneration for the holiness of the life she lives, as well as her intercessory role in approaching her son and our savior, Jesus Christ.

Yet Mary is not a static, one-dimensional figure for us. There are literally hundreds of images and names for Mary that attest to the depth of her person historically and the multi-dimensional aspects that the faithful focus upon. In fact, two entire works from Franciscan Media—*100 Names of Mary: Stories & Prayers,* by Anthony F. Chiffolo, and *Images of Mary,* by Alfred McBride—reflect that diversity.

Pope Paul VI, in his 1975 apostolic exhortation on Mary, *Marialis Cultus* (To Honor Mary), warned that our approach to Mary must not reflect outdated ideas of the Middle Ages and the Counter-Reformation period of the Church, views of Mary that are unappealing to contemporary people. He named, for example, the way that some theology presented Mary as timidly submissive and said that this is repellent to the piety of modern women.

Then he said the Church is not bound to these older images of Mary, some of which are showing the ravages of time. He pointed to five characteristics our understanding should include. These would be: (1) biblical, rooted in the testimony of Scripture; (2) liturgical, in tune with the great liturgical seasons; (3) ecumenical, in harmony with the agreements we have reached with fellow Christian churches; (4) anthropological, aware of the changing role of women in society and not, for instance, present Mary as a passive and subservient woman; and, (5) theological, with God at the center and Mary placed in relation to Christ and to the Church.

"Here Is Your Mother"
References to Mary in the Scriptures are not very abundant. And yet these passages give us not only a rich sense of the Mother of Jesus but also of her important role as Mother of the Church.

When Jesus said to his mother on Calvary, "Woman, here is your son" and to the disciple, "Here is your mother" (John 19:26–27), Jesus is doing more than entrusting his mother to John and John to her. He is making her mother of all the faithful. The beloved disciple here is seen as a symbol of all the disciples, indeed, a symbol of the whole Church. Mary is given a special role in the birth and development of all the redeemed.

Jesus's brief statement to his mother from the cross was like the reading of a will, for in an oral culture the last testament is spoken before a person dies and in the presence of witnesses. But he was also the savior and wished to involve his mother actively in the process of salvation.

Mary as "God-Bearer"
St. Paul expresses his supreme fascination with the fact that the Son of God had a mother: "But when the fullness of time had come, God

sent his Son, born of a woman…so that we might receive adoption as children" (Galatians 4:4–5). It did not have to be this way; Jesus could have just "appeared" on earth like the Old Testament priest-king Melchizedek, who was "Without father, without mother, without genealogy, having neither beginning of days nor end of life" (Hebrews 7:3). But God the Father intentionally and purposefully gave his Son a mother in the Incarnation. Why?

In his catechesis on Mary (*Theotokos: Mary, Mother of God*), Pope John Paul II said that Mary "has been granted an utterly special likeness between her motherhood and the divine fatherhood." The Father's gift of the motherhood of Mary can, in a way, be linked to the Eucharist. The maternity of Mary becomes a unique means by which we are able to receive the Self of Jesus Christ more perfectly. God gives a mother to his Son for us. Whatever makes God seem abstract, distant, aloof, elusive, unapproachable, or intimidating is overcome in a mother. Although the theology of Mary's maternity is rich and complex, its meaning becomes clear as we consider our own experiences.

The child Jesus does not enter the world apart from Mary his Blessed Mother, the *Theotokos*. In her pilgrimage of faith, hope and love she blazes the trail on which the Church is to follow. She continues to go before the people of God, as Pope John Paul II wrote in the encyclical *Redemptoris Mater* (6, 25, 28), coming to the help of those who seek to rise above their sins and misery.

Mary's Role in Her Son's "First Sign"

During the wedding feast at Cana, Jesus, in what was "the first of his signs" (John 2:11) of working wonders in God's name, changed water into wine. The evangelist writes that Jesus "revealed his glory; and his disciples believed in him" (John 2:11).

And it is at this momentous event we see Mary's motherly intervention. With two brief statements, Mary exerts a distinct influence on her son. First is the simple observation, "They have no wine," to which Jesus replies, "Woman, what concern is that to you and to me? My hour has not yet come." Jesus shows resistance to the clear drift of her words. Mary dispelled any hesitation about the "hour" and says to the attendants: "Do whatever he tells you" (John 2:3–5).

Her faith moved her to ask Jesus to begin manifesting his saving presence and public ministry of love. His heavenly Father had initiated him for ministry at the Jordan baptism. His earthly mother interceded with him at Cana to begin that ministry by performing a sign. She wanted his messianic work to be revealed. Jesus perfectly understood what she meant. Their communion as mother and son assured that kind of understanding.

When Mary again heard her son call her "woman" at the cross, she recalled that formal beginning of the salvation process at Cana. The two settings—Cana and Calvary, the wedding and the deathbed—are like an altarpiece, twin art works that belong together and have a unified message. Cana invites us to think of Mary as an intercessor. Calvary moves us to invoke her as our mother.

Mary in the Upper Room at the Church's Birth

The second time we see Mary at intercessory prayer is in the Upper Room with the 120 disciples of Jesus during the nine-day "novena" before Pentecost.

As the apostles and other men and women prepared for their mission, Mary stood with them and prayed. They gazed on the mother of Jesus and felt the special presence of a woman who was a unique witness to the mystery of Jesus from the moment of his conception.

Just as Mary was present at the conception and birth of Jesus, so she was present at the birth of the Church. As she bore Jesus in her womb and nurtured him, so she is to help bear the Church into life and holiness. The prayer group in the Upper Room experienced the unbreakable bond of Jesus and Mary. As the Church came to birth, its members stood next to Mary, the first believer in Jesus.

Mary believed long before anyone else: at Nazareth, at Bethlehem, at the Temple, during Jesus's public ministry, and at the cross, where, like Abraham, she hoped against hope. Her faith did not fail at the cross. As Abraham became the father of faith for the people of the first covenant, Mary became the mother of faith for the members of the Christian covenant.

At Pentecost Mary stood with those who would be the seed of the new Church, witnessing to them that her own long pilgrimage of faith was a model for what lay ahead. Mary had been present at all the key events in the process of salvation from Nazareth to Pentecost.

Mary: Model of Love

Jesus gave us Mary to be our spiritual mother. We have seen that she is a witness to faith and prayer for us. She is also a teacher of love.

Mary decided to love. Mary faced the mystery of conceiving a child without having a husband. Simply and honestly she asked the angel how this could happen. She was not closed-minded or paralyzed because of the mystery. Humanly speaking, she just wanted to know.

God gave her a supernatural answer. The Holy Spirit would make it happen. That was enough for her. She made a love decision and accepted God's word. She bore a child not as a result of a human love act, but a divine love deed.

As she played a key role in humankind's redemption and the coming reign of God, whose intent was to heal, redeem, and liberate, it does no honor to reduce her faith to a privatized piety. Worse yet, which sometimes happens in traditional Mariology, is to reduce her faith to a doting mother-son relationship.

She hears the word of God and keeps it. And in this too she is, as Paul VI called her in *Marialis Cultus*, our sister in faith. With a heart full of love for God and for her neighbor, Mary of Nazareth gives us this tremendous example of walking by faith through a difficult life.

The historical Mary experienced poverty, oppression, violence, and the execution of her son. Her faith is deeply rooted in that context. Before the omnipotent God, she recognizes her own "lowly estate." She is not among the world's powerful. She is simply God's "maidservant." But she believes that nothing is impossible for God. In the Magnificat, she sings confidently that God rescues life from death, joy from sorrow, light from darkness.

As reported in Luke's Gospel, Mary cries out with gratitude for God's gifts, especially for the son in her womb: "My soul magnifies the Lord, and my spirit rejoices in God my Savior" (Luke 1:46–47). She believes that, in Jesus, the power of God can turn the world upside down, ushering in a new era, a kingdom of justice, love, and peace: "He has brought down the powerful from their thrones, and lifted up the lowly" (Luke 1:52).

Dietrich Bonhoeffer, the theologian-martyr executed by the Nazis in 1945, said of the Magnificat during a sermon in 1933: "The song of Mary is the oldest Advent hymn. It is at once the most passionate, the wildest, one might even say the most revolutionary Advent hymn ever sung. This is not the gentle, tender, dreamy Mary whom we sometimes see in paintings; this is that passionate, surrendered, proud, enthusiastic Mary who speaks out here. This song has none of the sweet, nostalgic, or even playful tones of some of our Christmas carols. It is instead a hard, strong, inexorable song about collapsing thrones and humbled lords of this world, about the power of God and the powerless of humankind."

Questions for Reflection

1. Why did Jesus, while on the cross, say of Mary, "Here is your mother?"
2. How is Mary a model of love?
3. What are examples of Mary's active presence in her son's ministry?

CHAPTER FOUR

Feasts of Mary

The various celebrations of Mary are scattered throughout the year. Because these feast days do not occur within the calendar in the same order that the events actually happened in Mary's life, their relationship to the story of Jesus and Mary can sometimes be lost. When we read them in the "living" order in which they happened, we can more easily appreciate Mary's faith journey as well as the relationship of these feasts to Jesus's life.

As the Second Vatican Council reminded us, we honor Mary when we celebrate the cycle of Christ's saving mysteries. "Mary is joined by an inseparable bond to the saving work of her Son" (Constitution on the Sacred Liturgy, 107).

The Immaculate Conception: December 8

This feast is not the commemoration of Jesus's conception (as is sometimes thought) but of Mary's. Although Joachim and Anne are not named in the Bible, an ancient tradition holds that they were Mary's parents. Their feast is on July 26. We believe that Mary was conceived by her parents in the natural human way, but that she was conceived without original sin. This is a gift God gave her in anticipation of her Son's redemption.

When Pope Pius IX defined this belief in 1854, he explained that God's grace was given to her "in such a wonderful manner that she would always be free from every stain of sin." Mary is revered as patroness of the United States under this title.

The Birth of Mary: September 8

Although we do not know the date of Mary's birth, Christians have celebrated it on this day since the seventh century. The date of the feast of the Immaculate Conception was determined by counting back nine months from this date, the time from conception to birth. Mary's birthday is one of only three celebrated in the Christian calendar. Along with the births of John the Baptist and Jesus, it celebrates the dawn of salvation.

The Presentation of Mary in the Temple: November 21

Once again, we have no New Testament record of this event, but we do know that Mary's presentation was celebrated in Jerusalem in the sixth century. The feast is associated with an event recounted in the apocryphal Protoevangelium of James, which tells us that Anne and Joachim offered Mary to God in the Temple when she was three years old. This was to carry out a promise made to God when Anne was still childless.

Though it cannot be proven historically, Mary's presentation has an important theological purpose. It emphasizes that the holiness conferred on Mary from the beginning of her life on earth continued through her early childhood and beyond.

The Annunciation: March 25

All of the most important feasts of Mary are really celebrations of Jesus. That is why the name of this feast was changed from the

Annunciation of Mary to the Annunciation of Our Lord. It is the celebration of Jesus's conception by the Virgin Mary, accomplished by the power of the Holy Spirit. The Gospel reading for this feast, Luke 1:26–38, is the first time Mary appears in the Bible.

The angel Gabriel greets her with the words that have become the first part of the Hail Mary. Mary is deeply disturbed and fearful. Yet she places her trust in God, saying, "I am the handmaid of the Lord. May it be done to me according to your word." Once again we see that the feast of Jesus's conception occurs exactly nine months before the celebration of his birth. When March 25 falls during Holy Week, the Annunciation is celebrated after Easter.

The Visitation: May 31

Luke's account of the Annunciation is immediately followed by his story of Mary's visit to her cousin Elizabeth, who despite her advanced age was soon to be the mother of John the Baptist (Luke 1:39–56). This date is after the Annunciation but before the celebration of John's birth on June 24 so that the order of these days in our liturgy follows the actual order of the events.

Elizabeth greets Mary with the words that are the second part of the Hail Mary: "Blessed are you among women, and blessed is the fruit of your womb" (Luke 1:42). In response, Mary offers a prayer that is known today as the Magnificat (Luke 1:46–55): "My soul magnifies the Lord." The name of the prayer comes from the Latin word *magnificat*, which is the first word of the prayer, sometimes translated as "My soul proclaims the greatness of the Lord."

The Birth of Jesus: December 25
Advent presents Mary, Isaiah, and John the Baptist as models for our preparation for the coming of Jesus. The Gospel for the fourth Sunday of Advent particularly focuses on Mary's role in God's plan of salvation. While the celebration of Christmas naturally focuses on Jesus, we reflect also on Mary's part in giving him life and upon her vital link to the whole mystery of the Incarnation.

The Solemnity of Mary, the Mother of God: January 1
This is the oldest and most important feast of Mary. Coming one week after Christmas, it is a second celebration of Jesus's birth with a special focus on Mary as the Mother of God. The title "Mother of God" was given to Mary at the Council of Ephesus in 431. In the early Church some claimed that Mary should only be called the mother of the human Jesus and not the Mother of God. The council taught, however, that the humanity and divinity of Jesus could not be separated, and that they exist in the one person with the momentous implication.

The Presentation of the Lord: February 2
The Feast of the Presentation of Jesus in the Temple was previously called the Purification of Mary, but its name was changed to place the focus more clearly on Jesus. Yet because of Mary's role in these events, it is still a day to reflect on her. In the Gospel, we hear the prophecy of Simeon spoken to her, "so that the inner thoughts of many will be revealed—and a sword will pierce your own soul too" (Luke 2:35). Pope John Paul II, in his encyclical letter, Mother of the Redeemer (1987), in reflecting on these words, said "This announcement…reveals to her that she will have to live her obedience of faith in suffering at the side of the suffering Savior."

Mary in the Life of Jesus

While there are no specific celebrations of Mary to highlight her role in Jesus's life after his birth, we do encounter her at various times throughout the Church's year. On the feast of the Holy Family, we hear the Gospel account of Mary and Joseph finding Jesus in the Temple. On the second Sunday in Ordinary Time, we see her with Jesus at the wedding feast of Cana, urging him to do something to help the couple whose wine has run out. On Passion Sunday and Good Friday, we find Mary at the foot of the cross, fulfilling the prophecy that Simeon spoke when Jesus was just an infant. And on Pentecost, Luke reminds us that Mary was with the apostles in the Upper Room when the Holy Spirit came upon them.

The Assumption: August 15

We do not know anything about Mary's life after Pentecost. Christian tradition holds that Mary spent the last years of her life in Ephesus (in present-day Turkey) with the apostle John. The Assumption of the Blessed Virgin Mary refers to the bodily taking up of the Virgin Mary into heaven at the end of her earthly life. Pope Pius XII asserted as dogma in his 1950 Apostolic Constitution *Munificentissimus Deus* that Mary "having completed the course of her earthly life, was assumed body and soul into heavenly glory."

Six Marian Celebrations of Special Interest

In addition to the celebrations of Mary's life, there are six other celebrations of her in the liturgical calendar for the United States. Although there are many other titles by which we venerate Mary, we focus here only on those that we celebrate in the liturgy.

The Immaculate Heart of Mary: Date varies
This feast was extended to the universal Church by Pius XII in 1944. The celebration of this day varies according to the date of Easter, usually taking place in June on the Saturday after the feast of the Sacred Heart of Jesus. The hearts of Jesus and Mary are often depicted together as an expression of their union in love and their love for us. This day reminds us of Mary's sinlessness, of the prayerful way she pondered the mystery of Jesus in her heart, and of her unceasing love for us.

Our Lady of Mt. Carmel: July 16
Mt. Carmel is located on the coast of Israel just north of the city of Haifa. Tradition holds that it was the place where the prophet Elijah confronted the pagan prophets of Baal (see 1 Kings 18:19–46). It is also the site of an ancient shrine of Mary and where the Order of Our Lady of Mt. Carmel was founded about 1154. This contemplative order, known as the Carmelites, began to celebrate its patronal feast on July 16 because, according to its tradition, it was on this day in 1251 that Mary appeared to the Carmelite St. Simon Stock in England and gave him the brown scapular as a sign of her love and protection.

The Dedication of St. Mary Major: August 5
The Basilica of St. Mary Major is located in Rome on one of the seven hills of the city. It is one of the most ancient churches in Rome and the first among the churches dedicated to Mary. On this day, we celebrate Mary as Mother and Model of the Church.

The Queenship of Mary: August 22
Following the establishment of the feast of Christ the King, Pope Pius XII created this feast in 1954 on May 31. The new calendar moved it to August 22 to emphasize its connection with the Assumption. We venerate Mary as queen for two reasons: because of her unique part in redemption and because she is first among the saints. As Pius XII said of her: "Like her Son before her, she conquered death and was raised body and soul into heaven, where as queen, she sits in splendor at the right hand of her Son."

Our Lady of Sorrows: September 15
One aspect of Mary's life that is being appreciated anew today is her suffering and her connection with the poor, with refugees, as a mother whose son is unjustly murdered, and as a widow. The Gospels give us ample record of the suffering Mary endured. The circumstances of Jesus's birth were harsh, even by the standards of the day. Afterward the Holy Family fled to Egypt to escape persecution by Herod. The loss of Jesus in the Temple signaled the new challenge of understanding his ministry. Ultimately, his passion and death were her greatest trial.

Our Lady of the Rosary: October 7
The origins of this feast lie in the sixteenth century, when the Christian armies of Europe won a number of victories over the Muslim Turks. While the battles raged, the people of Rome prayed the rosary. In thanksgiving for the victory of the Christian navies at Lepanto, October 7, 1571, the day was dedicated to Our Lady of Victory, which was soon changed to Our Lady of the Rosary. Catholics today do not celebrate this victory, but rather give thanks

for the gift of the rosary. Because of this feast, the month of October has been dedicated to the rosary.

Two Feasts Linked with Apparitions

Two more days exist in our calendar of Marian celebrations: Our Lady of Lourdes and Our Lady of Guadalupe. These commemorate only two of the many reported apparitions of Mary to be found in the liturgical calendar for the United States. Although devotion to Our Lady of Fatima is popular among many groups in this country, the Fatima (Portugal) apparitions of 1917, though recognized by the universal Church, are not celebrated as an official, nationwide feast in the U.S. liturgical calendar. There are many other apparitions that enjoy the Church's approval, but they are celebrated, for the most part, only in those areas of the world where they occurred.

Our Lady of Lourdes: February 11

On this date in 1858, the Blessed Mother appeared to a fourteen-year-old girl named Bernadette Soubirous. This was the first of eighteen apparitions. When Bernadette was pressed by the local abbot to learn the name of the woman who was appearing to her, Mary identified herself as "the Immaculate Conception." Since the dogma had only recently been proclaimed and was unknown to Bernadette, the message was convincing.

The apparitions were given the Church's approval in 1862. In the years that followed, many came to this small French town in the Pyrenees and were healed in the waters flowing from a spring that welled up in the grotto where the apparitions took place. The pilgrimages and healings continue today.

Our Lady of Guadalupe: December 12
In December of 1531, Our Lady appeared to an Aztec farmer named Juan Diego near a native Aztec shrine in Tepeyac, near present-day Mexico City. She told Juan to go to the bishop and ask that a church be built in that place. When the bishop demanded a sign, Mary instructed Juan to take with him the roses that were blooming there, even though it was December.

Returning to the bishop's house, Juan removed his coarse cloak and found that the image of Our Lady was emblazoned upon it. The cloak with its image is still viewed today inside the Basilica of Our Lady of Guadalupe by pilgrims from around the world. Our Lady of Guadalupe, who was declared "Patroness of the Americas" by Pope Pius XII in 1954, is widely revered throughout our hemisphere and receives special affection from Native American and Hispanic communities.

Questions for Reflection

1. How is the Annunciation related to the Visitation?
2. What is the gift associated with the feast of the Immaculate Conception?
3. What do the different images of Mary tell us about her life and presence in the Church today?

CHAPTER FIVE

Praying the Rosary

For many Catholics in the past, the rosary represented their primary way of praying alone or as a family, and, in fact, became a vehicle to bring families together.

"From my childhood," writes Thomas Groome, professor of theology and religious education at Boston College, in *Catholic Spiritual Practices,* "I knew the rosary as both communal and personal prayer, as a quieting mantra-like mode of recitation and contemplation. It convinced me that we can go to Jesus through Mary, and that a great communion of saints prays with us. It taught me the responsibility of praying by myself as well as with others; it taught me that I could pray just about any time and any place."

The rosary suffered a slow decline for a period of time after the Second Vatican Council. Some scholars have suggested that it was seen as too mechanical, a relic of the past, eclipsing the Eucharist as the central focus of Catholic life.

The reemergence of the rosary has been propelled by Pope John Paul II's 2002 apostolic letter *Rosarium Virginis Mariae* (The Rosary of the Virgin Mary). In the letter's introduction, John Paul II emphasizes that, though we pray for Mary's intercession, the rosary is truly about

Jesus. It is "at heart a Christo-centric prayer" that can be seen as a short summary of the Gospel.

It is in the apostolic letter that the Holy Father introduced five new mysteries—the luminous mysteries (mysteries of light)—to be added to the traditional fifteen that focus respectively on Christ's childhood (joyful mysteries), on his suffering and death (sorrowful mysteries), and on his resurrection and the events that follow it (glorious mysteries). In making this change, the pope propelled the rosary to fill the void in Jesus's biography that jumped from birth to death without his ministry on earth and with his disciples.

Praise from the Popes

Paul VI was another pope who found great value in the rosary. In a 1974 document, he wrote, "the rosary is an excellent prayer," adding "the faithful should be serenely free toward it. Its intrinsic appeal should draw them to calm recitation" (On Devotion to the Blessed Virgin, 55).

Pope John Paul II, as has been noted, also was a staunch advocate of the rosary. In June of 1987—by way of a live satellite telecast in which millions participated from five continents—he celebrated the opening of the Marian year by praying the rosary with the faithful from around the world.

When the same pope survived an assassin's bullet in St. Peter's Square in 1981 on the sixty-fourth anniversary of the first appearance of Our Lady to the children at Fatima, he credited his safety to the protection of Mary and expressed his gratitude by way of the rosary. On the day the pope resumed his public appearances, October 7 (the Feast of the Holy Rosary), he pointed out the connection with Fatima, saying he was "indebted to the Blessed Virgin" and adding, "the holy rosary is and always remains a prayer of gratitude, love and trustful request: the prayer of the Mother of the Church."

"Simple yet profound, it still remains," Pope John Paul said in *Rosarium Virginis Mariae*, "a prayer of great significance, destined to bring forth a harvest of holiness."

The rosary, he continued, "blends easily into the spiritual journey of the Christian life, which, after two thousand years, has lost none of the freshness of its beginnings. It is an echo of the prayer of Mary, her perennial Magnificat for the work of the redemptive Incarnation, which began in her virginal womb," he said, adding, "the rosary is my favorite prayer, marvelous in its simplicity and its depth."

Roots of the Rosary

Where did this popular devotion come from that has enabled it to remain, for more than nine centuries, a prayer for all seasons?

The historical particulars are hard to pin down. But the custom of praying with a string of beads was already common in the twelfth century. Buddhists, Sikhs, and Muslims had long used beads to count certain prayers that were repeated. Christian monks ran beads or knotted string through their fingers as they chanted their required 150 psalms. This led some common folk to resourcefully praying 150 Our Fathers on the beads as their version of the monks' prayer.

Any account of how the rosary developed has to pause and make a respectful bow to St. Dominic (1170–1221) and the Order of Preachers, which he founded. While accounts of Dominic actually receiving the rosary from Mary during an apparition are difficult to substantiate, most historians believe the rosary developed slowly during a timespan stretching possibly from the 1100s to 1569, when Pope Pius V officially approved the devotion. However, the saint and his followers certainly propagated the prayer from the thirteenth century onward.

One measure of the prayer's early popularity is the jealous infighting among religious orders to claim it as their own. Both St. Francis of Assisi and St. Ignatius were, at various times, credited as the recipients of Our Lady's rosary. To stake their respective claims, members of these religious orders commissioned paintings of Mary passing the rosary to Francis or Ignatius. Not to be outdone, the Dominicans convinced the pope to ban any art depicting anyone but their founder receiving, in his outstretched hands, the coveted string of beads from Mary.

The rosary took its present form between the fourteenth and fifteenth centuries. A Carthusian monk divided the 150 *Ave Marias* into the fifteen decades, with each decade preceded by the Lord's Prayer.

The rosary took the form familiar to us today in the sixteenth century. Pope Pius V recommended that Catholics pray on their beads 150 Hail Marys in decades separated by an Our Father, while reflecting on the life of Christ. Pius left his distinctive mark on the prayer by adding the second half of the Hail Mary to the biblical beginning (Luke 1:28, 42).

Having endured the centuries with varying degrees of fidelity paid to it, the rosary has always been seen as a prayer of the people. It has been described as "a garland of roses" (the meaning of its name), "a string of pearls" (poet Robert Cameron Rogers), and "one harp that any hand can play" (poet Joyce Kilmer). Pope Paul VI even referred to the rosary as a Bible for those unable to read.

With time, mysteries from the life of Christ were added to give those praying material for contemplation and to keep Christ as the central focus of the devotion.

For the next four hundred years, the rosary remained unchanged, until the introduction of the five new luminous mysteries. During almost a century and a half—from Pope Leo XIII (1878–1903) to the present—this prayer has been consistently and highly recommended by the popes.

The Luminous Mysteries: The Missing Link

When Pope John Paul II issued his apostolic letter *Rosarium Virginis Mariae* and introduced the new "Mysteries of Light," he shined light on the centuries-old gap in the whole public ministry of Jesus between his youth in the last joyful mystery (the finding of the twelve-year-old Jesus in the Temple) and the first sorrowful mystery (Jesus's agony in the garden the night before his death). The Holy Father's primary purpose in adding the five mysteries of light to the rosary was to make the prayer "more fully a compendium of the Gospel" (*Rosarium Virginis Mariae*, 21).

The five new mysteries begin with the Baptism of Jesus (spotlighting his identity as God's beloved Son and his mission as the messiah). The Baptism is followed by the Wedding at Cana (illuminating the first sign Jesus gave of his yet-to-be-revealed glory) and the Proclamation of the Kingdom (holding a bright candle to Jesus's saving work of healing and forgiveness).

These three mysteries are followed by the Transfiguration (the most luminous of the mysteries, in which Jesus's glory and divine nature shine) and the First Eucharist (enlightening our understanding of Jesus's self-gift to us at the Last Supper, as well as our identity as the one Body of Christ).

Although Mary remains in the background of four of the mysteries of light, she stands forth as an intercessor in the Wedding at Cana. Her words to the wine steward may be taken as her counsel to the Church in every season: "Do whatever he tells you" (John 2:5). As the Holy Father points out: "This counsel is a fitting introduction to the words and signs of Christ's public ministry and it forms the Marian foundation of all the mysteries of light'" (*Rosarium Virginis Mariae,* 21).

A Gospel Prayer

A quick look at the structure of the rosary shows it to be truly a Scripture-based prayer drawing especially upon the Gospels. The Apostles' Creed itself, leading off the rosary, is nothing other than a summary of the great mysteries of the Catholic faith, most of which are standard Gospel teachings. Each decade is preceded by the Our Father, a prayer straight from the Gospels and taught by Jesus himself as a model of all prayer.

The first part of the Hail Mary is composed of verses from the Gospel of Luke (1:28 and 1:42): the angel's words announcing Christ's birth and Elizabeth's greeting to Mary. Both of these Gospel passages are rich in meaning and point to the central mystery of our faith, the incarnation of the messiah.

The angel's greeting to Mary is one of joy announcing the "breakthrough" of a new age: "Rejoice, God's favored one, the Lord is with you." At the moment of the Annunciation, Mary—the Daughter of Zion and the Mother of the Church—represents both those who have awaited the Savior and those who now accept him in faith.

Mary's key role in the mystery of Christ is not a rosary invention. Rather, it is a vital part of the Gospel that is simply reflected in the rosary. The sense of the faithful that the rosary is a prayer of confidence in Mary's love and intercession for us is rooted in the Good News of the Gospel.

The Gospel passages from which the Hail Mary was drawn, moreover, reveal the virgin as a dynamic, grace-filled woman to whom God offered a pivotal and active role in the drama of salvation.

Paul VI called the attention of modern women to the reality that the Mary we hail in the *Ave Maria* was a dynamic, grace-filled woman who gave her "active and responsible consent" to the Incarnation. When she proclaimed her radical Magnificat, she announced God's vindication of the oppressed against the powerful and privileged of this world (Devotion to the Blessed Virgin Mary, 37).

Those who picture her as a passive woman uninvolved in the work of forging God's kingdom of justice and peace have not yet encountered the Mary of the Gospels. They have yet to reconcile their malleable Mary with the prophetic one who rejoices in the downfall of the mighty and the lifting up of the lowly.

If the rosary is truly to reflect the spirit of the Gospel and that of the Virgin Mary as portrayed there, then it must encourage, among other things, dynamic responsibility on the part of both women and men as well as a commitment to walking with God's poor.

A Christ-Centered Prayer

The mysteries of the rosary are clearly centered on events in Christ's life—the joyful mysteries on his incarnation, the luminous mysteries on his public ministry, the sorrowful mysteries on his suffering and death, and the glorious mysteries on his resurrection. "In praying the rosary with devotion," said Mother Teresa of Calcutta, "we are reliving the life of Christ."

The mysteries of Christ (and Mary) do not simply refer to past events. Christ truly lives among us now, continuing to be born, to suffer, die, and rise again in the Church of our day. When we pray, "Blessed is the fruit of thy womb, Jesus," we need to remember that we, too, the body of Christ, are also the fruit of her womb, for we are born of the Christ who was born of Mary. Mary is not only the Mother of Christ, but also the Mother of the Church, whom Pope Paul VI described as "the new Eve...cooperating in the birth and development of divine life in the souls of the redeemed" (quoted by Pope John Paul II in Mother of the Redeemer, 47).

A Tool for Contemplation

The rosary is meant to be a prayer that leads us to Christ and into union with God. If it only locks us into a meaningless circle of mechanically recited prayers, the rosary is not achieving its purpose. And Mary would be the first one to tell us to find a better way to God and love of neighbor.

The words of the rosary are meant to launch us into the mysteries of Christ's life or, better, into the living mystery of Christ himself, who says, "I am with you always even until the end of time." Just as each Hail Mary builds up to the word Jesus, so the whole rosary leads to union with him. And through Jesus we come into union with the Triune God. Each decade ends with "Glory be to Father, to the Son, and to the Holy Spirit…" suggesting that the whole rosary is a movement toward praise and joyful union with God.

In praying the rosary, it's important not to get too tied down or worried about the words, at least, not to get anxious about them. If you feel inspired to savor the words and their meaning, that's fine. There is a scriptural richness and a spiritual energy to be tapped from the words themselves. But don't hesitate to soar beyond the words to the mysteries of Christ or into the loving presence of God. If distracting thoughts come and your mind drifts to last night's dinner, to a movie, or to personal problems, that's OK. Be at peace. Gently move back to the words or mysteries or talk to Jesus about your distractions.

As mentioned above, it's not always necessary to focus on the words. More important is to pray from the heart. Many people who say the rosary consider the words to be like background music leading them more deeply into the mysteries or into God's loving presence within. The gentle murmur of the words, for example, can take us into that silent center within us where Jesus's Spirit dwells as in a temple.

The use of repetition as a tool for contemplation is an ancient practice. Repeating a sacred word or verses of Scripture, in rhythm with one's breathing perhaps, is a method of contemplative prayer described by early Christian writers and which survives today in various forms of centering prayer. Other religious traditions, such as Hinduism, use mantras—the repeating of sacred words—as an aid to contemplation.

Using beads during prayers is also a custom common in other religious traditions, such as among Buddhists and Muslims. Just as the repetition of words and breathing can lead to a contemplative state, so also can the soothing repetition of touch. The use of beads brings the sense of touch into the act, making the rosary a prayer of the body as well as of the mind. It's also a way of bringing creation itself (wood, metal, glass, artwork) into the service of God—a very incarnational way of praying.

Breathing Life into Your Prayer

Here are a few simple suggestions about how to remain "at home" with God no matter where you're praying the rosary. First, take time to relax and breathe deeply from your diaphragm before beginning to pray, as if you are breathing life into your prayer. Then ease into the prayer while remaining in touch with the steady rhythm of the Spirit breathing and praying in you.

Decide to reflect on one mystery at a time with the undivided attention usually reserved for loved ones who have been away too long. The same approach can be used for each of the consecutive four mysteries. You can get through an entire decade this way. Be patient with yourself if distractions come. Gently let them go and move back to the mystery at hand.

You may find it helpful to pray a mystery that connects most closely with your life at that particular time. For instance, when facing a difficult decision or wondering what direction God wants you to take, ponder the Baptism of the Lord. Connect with Jesus as he leaves his earlier life behind and emerges from the Jordan to do the work of God's Beloved Son.

Or when the comfort and predictability of your life are suddenly disrupted by some unexpected but demanding opportunity, ponder the Annunciation. Connect with Mary as the blessed disturbance of Gabriel's message—and her daring yes—turn her young life upside down and sideways.

More important than any suggestions, tools, or techniques for praying the rosary is the conviction that God treasures each word, each thought, each quiet pondering in which our hearts are invested. And the more practiced we become at staying "at home" with our loving God, the more meaningful the rosary will become in our daily lives.

How to Pray the Rosary

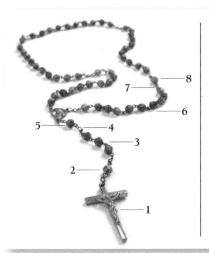

1. Make the Sign of the Cross and pray the Apostles' Creed.
2. Pray the Our Father.
3. Pray three Hail Marys.
4. Pray the Glory Be.
5. Announce the mystery for reflection and pray the Our Father.
6. Pray 10 Hail Marys.
7. Finish the decade with the Glory Be.
8. Repeat this process (5,6,7) for each decade.

The Mysteries of the Rosary

The Joyful Mysteries (Mondays and Saturdays)

1. The Annunciation to Mary that She Is to Be the Mother of the Savior (Luke 1:26–38).
2. The Visitation of Mary to Her Cousin Elizabeth (Luke 1:39–47).
3. The Nativity of Our Lord Jesus Christ (Luke 2:1–7).
4. The Presentation of the Infant Jesus in the Temple (Luke 2:22–32).
5. The Finding of the Child Jesus in the Temple (Luke 2:41–52).

The Luminous Mysteries (Thursdays)

1. The Baptism of Jesus in the Jordan (Matthew 3:17).
2. The Wedding Feast at Cana (John 2:1–12).

3. The Proclamation of the Kingdom of God/The Call to Conversion (Mark 1:15; Mark 2:3–13; Luke 7:47–48; John 20:22–23).
4. The Transfiguration (Luke 9:35).
5. The First Eucharist (John 13:1).

The Sorrowful Mysteries (Tuesdays and Fridays)
1. The Agony of Christ in the Garden (Mark 14:32–36).
2. The Scourging of Jesus at the Pillar (John 18:28–38; 19:1).
3. The Crowning with Thorns (Mark 15:16–20).
4. The Carrying of the Cross (John 19:12–16).
5. The Crucifixion and Death of Jesus (Luke 23:33–34; 39–46).

The Glorious Mysteries (Sundays and Wednesdays)
1. The Resurrection of Jesus (Luke 24:1–6).
2. The Ascension of Our Lord into Heaven (Luke 24:50–53).
3. The Descent of the Holy Spirit (Acts 2:1–4).
4. The Assumption of Mary into Heaven (Song of Songs 2:8–14).
5. The Coronation of Our Lady in Heaven (Revelation 12:1–6).

Questions for Reflection

1. Have you prayed the rosary? What is your experience of praying it alone or as a family?
2. How do the luminous mysteries shine a light on faith?
3. What is the Gospel story that the rosary and its twenty mysteries proclaim?

CHAPTER SIX

Other Prayers to Mary

Hail Mary

Hail Mary, full of grace, the Lord is with you. Blessed are you among women, and blessed is the fruit of your womb, Jesus. Holy Mary, Mother of God, pray for us sinners, now and at the hour of our death. Amen.

Angelus

V. The angel spoke God's message to Mary.
R. and she conceived of the Holy Spirit
Hail, Mary full of grace…
V. "I am the lowly servant of the Lord:
R. let it be done to me according to your word."
Hail, Mary full of grace…
V. And the Word became flesh
R. and lived among us.
Hail, Mary full of grace…
V. Pray for us, holy Mother of God,
R. that we may become worthy of the promises of Christ
Let us pray.

Loving God, fill our hearts with your grace: Once, through the message of an angel you revealed to us the incarnation of your Son; now, through his suffering and death lead us to the glory of his resurrection. We ask this through Christ our Lord. Amen.

Hail, Holy Queen
Hail, holy Queen, Mother of Mercy;
Our life, our sweetness, and our hope!
To you we cry, poor banished children of Eve.
To you we send up our sighs, mourning and weeping in this vale of tears.
Turn then, most gracious advocate, your eyes of mercy toward us;
And after this our exile, show unto us the blessed fruit of your womb, Jesus.
O clement, O loving, O sweet Virgin Mary.

Magnificat, or the Canticle of Mary (Luke 1:46–55)
My soul proclaims the greatness of the Lord,
my spirit rejoices in God my Savior
for he has looked upon his handmaid's lowliness;
behold, from now on will all ages call me blessed.
The Mighty One has done great things for me,
and holy is his Name.
His mercy is from age to age
To those who fear him.
He has shown might with his arm,
dispersed the arrogant of mind and heart.
He has thrown down the rulers from their thrones,
But lifted up the lowly.

The hungry he has filled with good things;
the rich he has sent away empty.
He has helped Israel his servant,
remembering his mercy,
according to his promise to our fathers,
to Abraham and his descendants forever.

Memorare

Remember, O most gracious Virgin Mary,
that never was it known that anyone who fled to your protection,
implored your help, or sought your intercession was left unaided.
Inspired with this confidence, I fly to you, O virgin of virgins, my Mother.
To you I come, before you I kneel, sinful and sorrowful.
O Mother of the Word Incarnate, despise not my petitions;
but in your mercy, hear and answer me.
Amen.

Salve Regina

Hail, Holy Queen enthroned above, O Maria!
Hail, Mother of mercy and of love, O Maria!
Triumph all ye cherubim!
Sing with us ye seraphim!
Heaven and earth resound the hymn!
Salve, salve, salve, Regina!
Our life, our sweetness here below, O Maria!
Our hope in sorrow and in woe, O Maria!
Triumph all ye cherubim!
Sing with us ye seraphim!

Heaven and earth resound the hymn!
Salve, salve, salve, Regina!
And when our last breath leaves us, O Maria!
Show us thy son Christ Jesus, O Maria!
Triumph all ye cherubim!
Sing with us ye seraphim!
Heaven and earth resound the hymn!
Salve, salve, salve, Regina!

Questions for Reflection

1. What are some of the similarities of the prayers of Mary?
2. What Marian prayer speaks most closely to your life and why?
3. In the Magnificat, Mary's soul proclaims God's greatness. What does your soul proclaim?

Sources

Cameron, Peter John, O.P., "Mary: Mother of God and Our Mother," *Catholic Update*, May 2010.

Carroll, Kathleen M. *A Mary Christmas*. Cincinnati: Franciscan Media, 2012.

Chiffolo, Anthony F. *100 Names of Mary: Stories & Prayers*. Cincinnati: St. Anthony Messenger Press, 2002.

Dulles, Avery, S.J., "Mary and the Millennium," *Catholic Update*, December 1998.

Hamma, Robert M., "The Feasts of Mary," *Catholic Update*, May 1992.

Hutchinson, Gloria, "The Rosary: A Prayer for All Seasons," *Catholic Update*, August 2003.

Johnson, Elizabeth, C.S.J., "In Search of the Real Mary," *Catholic Update*, May 2001.

Maloney, Robert P., C.M., "Mary of History," *Catholic Update*, May 2008.

McBride, Alfred, O.PRAEM. *Holding Jesus: Reflections on Mary the Mother of God*. Cincinnati: Franciscan Media, 2012.

———. *Images of Mary*. Cincinnati: St. Anthony Messenger Press, 1999.

———. "Mary of Nazareth: Jesus' Mother," *Catholic Update*, May 1991.

Pope John Paul II, "The Rosary of the Virgin Mary," *Catholic Update*, January 2003.

Sri, Edward, "The Annunciation: The Angel's Message to Mary," *Catholic Update*, December 2005.

Thompson, Thomas A., S.M., and Jack Wintz, O.F.M., "The Rosary: A Gospel Prayer," *Catholic Update*, May 1989.

Wintz, Jack, O.F.M., "The Luminous Mysteries: Exploring Five Major Events in Jesus' Public Ministry," *Catholic Update*, May 1989.

Contributors

Father Peter John Cameron, O.P., is the founding editor-in-chief of the monthly worship aid *Magnificat*. He is also the artistic director of Blackfriars Repertory Theater in New York City. His other books include *Mysteries of the Virgin Mary: Living Our Lady's Graces; The Classics of Catholic Spirituality; Why Preach: Encountering Christ in God's Word;* and *Jesus, Present Before Me: Meditations for Eucharistic Adoration.*

Kathleen M. Carroll is managing editor of the book department at Franciscan Media. She is the author of *A Franciscan Christmas; A Catholic Christmas; A Mary Christmas;* and *Keeping the Faith in Ohio: Words of Hope and Comfort from Our Spiritual Leaders*, and has written on a number of subjects for *Catholic Update*.

Anthony F. Chiffolo, a former naval officer, began a publishing career drawing upon his great interest in the mystical lives of the saints. He is the author of books on the saints including *100 Names of Mary: Stories & Prayers; At Prayer With the Saints; An Hour with Saint Thérèse of Lisieux; An Hour with Saint Padre Pio; Pope John Paul II: In My Own Words; Advent and Christmas With the Saints;* and *Be Mindful of Us: Prayers to the Saints.*

Cardinal Avery Dulles, S.J., was a professor of religion and society at Fordham University, the author of twenty-seven books and over eight hundred articles, a lecturer, and an elder statesman of Catholic theology in America. He was the only American theologian ever appointed to the College of Cardinals, named by Pope John Paul II in 2001. Cardinal Dulles served as president of the Catholic Theological Society of America and of the American Theological

Society. His books include *Models of the Church*, *The Reshaping of Catholicism,* and *The Splendor of Faith: The Theological Vision of Pope John Paul II.*

Robert M. Hamma is a bestselling author and the editorial director at Ave Maria Press and editor-in-chief for *Human Development.* He is the author of numerous books and articles on prayer, spirituality, and family life.

Gloria Hutchinson is a former teacher, catechist, author, and retreat director who writes extensively on the spiritual life. Her books include *Praying the Rosary; A Retreat With Teresa of Avila: Living by Holy Wit; Six Ways to Pray From Six Great Saints;* and *Praying the Way: Reflections on the Stations of the Cross.*

Elizabeth A. Johnson, C.S.J., is a distinguished professor of theology at Fordham University in New York, where she teaches in both undergraduate and graduate programs. A former president of both the Catholic Theological Society of America and American Theological Society, she is the author of books including *Quest for the Living God: Mapping Frontiers in Theology of God; Truly Our Sister: A Theology of Mary in the Communion of Saints; Friends of God and Prophets: A Feminist Theological Reading of the Communion of Saints;* and *Women, Earth, and Creator Spirit.*

Robert P. Maloney, C.M., the former superior general of the Congregation of the Mission, made extensive contributions to the understanding of the Vincentian charism. He has authored numerous articles and several books including *Go! On the Missionary Spirituality of St. Vincent de Paul; He Hears the Cry of the Poor: On the Spirituality of Vincent de Paul;* and *The Way of Vincent de Paul: A Contemporary Spirituality in the Service of the Poor.*

Alfred McBride, O.PRAEM., is the author of *Holding Jesus: Reflections on Mary, the Mother of God*; *The Challenge of the Cross: Praying the Stations*; *Staying Faithful Today: To God, Ourselves, One Another*; and *The Story of the Church*.

Edward Sri is a nationally known speaker and author and is a founder of Fellowship of Catholic University Students (FOCUS). He is the author of books including *The New Rosary in Scripture: Biblical Insights for Praying the 20 Mysteries*; *Dawn of the Messiah: The Coming of Christ in Scripture*; *Biblical Walk Through the Mass: Understanding What We Say and Do In The Liturgy*; and, *Men, Women and the Mystery of Love: Practical Insights from John Paul II's Love and Responsibility*.

Father Thomas Thompson, S.M., is director of the Marian Library at the University of Dayton and serves on the faculty of the International Research Institute and has served as secretary of the Mariological Society of America and editor of *Marian Studies* for more than twenty years.

Jack Wintz, O.F.M., is the senior editor of *Catholic Update* and editor emeritus of *St. Anthony Messenger* magazine. The Franciscan friar is the author of the electronic newsletter Friar Jack's E-Spirations, and books that include *Will I See My Dog in Heaven?*; *St. Anthony of Padua: His Life, Legends, and Devotions*; and *Friar Jack's Favorite Prayers*.